THE LITTLE BOOK OF

HOT
SAUCE

Published in 2023 by OH!
An imprint of Welbeck Non-Fiction Limited, part of Welbeck Publishing Group.
Offices in London, 20 Mortimer Street, London W1T 3JW,
and Sydney, 205 Commonwealth Street, Surry Hills 2010
www.welbeckpublishing.com

Text and Design © Welbeck Non-Fiction Limited 2023
Front cover: Bibadash/Shutterstock.
Cover design by Lucy Palmer

A CIP catalogue record for this book is available from the British Library.

ISBN 978-1-83861-140-8

Associate Publisher: Lisa Dyer
Compiled and written by: Theresa Bebbington
Design: Andy Jones, Topics – The Creative Partnership
Production: Felicity Awdry

Printed and bound in Dubai

10 9 8 7 6 5 4 3 2 1

THE LITTLE BOOK OF

HOT
SAUCE

A passionate salute to the world's
best-loved fiery condiments

Contents

Introduction

A connoisseur's guide to the best hot sauces around and ways to use them, as well as their main components, unique flavor profiles, and their heat levels, this little book will delight every chili aficionado.

Here you will find history and folklore, quotes and trivia, as well as the most popular brands and styles from around the world. Learn the different types of chilies and sauces, how to make spicy homemade condiments that are truly your own, and ways to fire up your food and tastebuds.

Chapter one, The Original Hot Sauces, takes you on a journey through the history of the hot sauce, from spice trade routes and family recipes to the first commercial brands created and distributed, such as the beloved world leader, Tabasco. Chapter two, Some Like It Hot, explains the different types of chilies, their flavor profiles, heat indexes, and complex and varied uses. Chapter three, Hot Sauces from Distant Places, is a global tour from Caribbean hot pepper sauce, Middle Eastern harissa, and Portuguese peri peri to Asian chili sauces and sriracha. Chapter four, A Love Affair with Hot Sauce, focuses on U.S. traditions, while chapter five, Homegrown and Homemade, explains how to grow and harvest chilies, and includes recipes for making your own fresh chili sauces—as well as tips on how to handle the hot stuff! Finally, chapter six, Make Mine Hot, features classic recipes with an extra kick for parties, family meals, snacks, and appetizers.

Whether you prefer a mild green salsa or the head-exploding superhot Mad Dog 357 Plutonium, are fanatical about your chilies or just a general foodie who needs to know it all, this little book offers detailed information and tantalizing recipes to get the most out of your favorite hot sauce.

Chapter 1

The Original Hot Sauces

Here's a look at the historical origins of hot sauce and the first inventions created in the Americas.

What Is Hot Sauce?

By combining three main ingredients—chilies, vinegar, and salt—and letting them ferment, you'll have a basic green, red, or brown hot sauce. However, despite being referred to as a "sauce," this chili-based condiment can be in a liquid or paste form. Of course, other ingredients can be added to the mix, but without chilies, spicy hot condiments such as mustard, horseradish, and wasabi don't count as a hot sauce!

The First Hot Sauce

No one is actually sure when the first hot sauce was enjoyed, but archaeological evidence dates back 1,700 to 2,400 years ago, with traces of capsaicin found in stoneware vessels. The first hot sauce was likely a combination of chilies, herbs, and water, and it is thought that it would have been used in food, medicine, and warfare (as a pepper spray).

Frogs with Green Chilies Please

A Spanish friar visiting the Americas in 1529 reported that chilies were used in almost all dishes, such as frogs with green chilies, newts with yellow chilies, and tadpoles with small chilies. While there's no record that these chilies were used in sauces, there's a chance that they were. These combinations may not be to your taste, but what about lobster with red chilies, another dish mentioned in his notes?

The First Advertisement for Hot Sauce

The first known advertisement for hot sauce appeared in Massachusetts in 1807 (making it more than 200 years old). It appeared in a city directory and was for a sauce made with cayenne peppers, bottled by a New Hampshire farmer. It is thought that the concoction was homemade rather than mass produced.

Tabasco, Mexico

It just so happens that a town in Mexico is called Tabasco, which, incidentally, is where the Spanish explorer Juan de Grijalva arrived in 1519. The word "tabasco" is of Mexican Indian origin, but the meaning is unclear; two suggestions are "place where the soil is humid" or "place of the coral or oyster shell." And, of course, one of the world's most popular chilies is named after this town.

Warfare Reward: Seeds

During the Mexican-American War of 1846–1848, American soldiers returning from Mexico brought with them the seeds from the tabasco chili plant. This was probably the first time spicy chilies were introduced to Louisiana, where they would soon be used to make Louisiana-style hot sauces (see page 23).

Sunken Treasure

The Missouri steamboat *Bertrand* sank in 1865, but when it was excavated, among the half a million artifacts discovered, there were a surprising 173 hot sauce bottles, produced by Western Spice Mills, based in St. Louis. This proves that bottles of hot sauce were already being sold in the Midwest before the Civil War.

"

The only really good vegetable is Tabasco sauce. Put Tabasco sauce in everything. Tabasco sauce is to bachelor cooking what forgiveness is to sin. The next best vegetable is the jalapeño pepper. It has the virtue of turning salads into practical jokes.

"

P. J. O'Rourke, political satirist and journalist

THE BEGINNING OF WHITE'S HOT SAUCE

The *New Orleans Daily Delta* newspaper reported in 1850 that Maunsel White was growing the tabasco red chili on a large scale, becoming the first recorded plantation of tabasco chilies. It described how he made a hot sauce:

". . . by pouring strong vinegar on it after boiling, he made a sauce or pepper decoction of it, which possesses in a most concentrated form all the qualities of the vegetable. A single drop of this sauce will flavor a whole plate of soup or other food."

The End of White's Hot Sauce

After Maunsel White's death, surviving family members tried their hand at selling his hot sauce, and an advertisement appeared in 1864 that described it as the "concentrated essence" of the tabasco chili. However, White's hot sauce wasn't the one that become America's iconic Tabasco; production ended within 20 years.

> 66

> *. . . they have hot peppers in Louisiana. Little red devils with fire in their skin and hell in their seeds.*

> 99

James Street, "The Grains of Paradise," *Saturday Evening Post*, May 1955

The Origins of McIlhenny's Hot Sauce

Edmund McIlhenny, who had been a banker before the Civil War, began growing tabasco chilies in 1865.

The process for making his first hot sauce has been described as mashing ripe red chilies with salt and letting them sit for a month, at which time a layer of mold was removed, and the chilies transferred to large jars with a wine vinegar. After another 30 days, a second layer of mold was removed before passing the mixture through sieves.

McIlhenny's First Bottled Sauce

When Edmund McIlhenny bottled his first hot sauce, it was called Petite Anse sauce, after the plantation on Avery Island that belonged to his wife's father. After a complaint from his father-in-law, the name was changed to Tabasco. In 1869, 658 cologne bottles were filled with Tabasco sauce and corked, to be sold to men's clubs and restaurants.

Louisiana Style

Original hot sauces could be recognized by their regional differences, because they were based on chefs using locally available ingredients and the preferred cooking styles of the area. McIlhenny's Tabasco sauce, Crystal hot sauce, Frank's RedHot, and Louisiana Original are all "Louisiana-style" hot sauces, noted for their tangy vinegary style.

Fighting Off the Competition

One of McIlhenny's former employees, B. F. Trappey, took some seeds from his old company and began growing his own tabasco chili plants in 1896. Other competitors also began selling their own versions. Edmund McIlhenny had obtained a patent for Tabasco in 1870, but it wasn't until 1906 that McIlhenny took out a trademark on the name—and from that point onward, only McIlhenny's sauce could be referred to as Tabasco sauce.

Still Here, Despite the Tabasco Ban

They may no longer be able to use the word "tabasco" for their products, but several hot sauces that began production in the 1920s are still on the market. These include Frank's RedHot cayenne pepper sauce, which is Jacob Frank's sauce that first appeared in New Iberia in 1920; Crystal hot sauce, the Baumer's family 1923 creation; and Original Louisiana hot sauce, first made in New Iberia, Louisiana, in 1928.

NOT JUST LOUISIANA STYLE

As well as the Louisiana-style hot sauces, other styles of hot sauces are popular, too. These may use different types of chilies, such as cayenne, chipotle, habanero, and jalapeño, as well as other ingredients, including fruit, vegetables, and flavorings, and the hot sauce can be garlicky or even sweet and sour.

New Mexico Style

A New Mexico-style hot sauce starts with a roux of red or green chilies as a base, using hatch, pueblo, or rio grande chilies, and skips on the vinegar. If you're dining out in New Mexico, expect your waitress or waiter to ask you if you prefer "the red" or "the green."

Frank's RedHot

Adam Estilette and Jacob Frank became partners when they create a hot sauce using cayenne chilies in 1918, but it wasn't until 1920 that the first bottle of Frank's RedHot was available. According to the company, there is only one original bottle still in existence.

Lucky Crystal

Alvin Baumer began producing Crystal hot sauce back in 1923 purely by chance. After the Civil War, he'd taken out a loan to purchase a syrup production company in New Orleans. While in the building, he opened a drawer, where he found a recipe for a hot sauce called Crystal Pure ... and the rest is history, with bottles of Crystal enjoyed as far away as Dubai.

Texas Pete Hot Sauce

Despite its name, Texas Pete hot sauce was first made in North Carolina. Sam Garner, the patriarch of the family behind this sauce, refused to name it Mexican Joe, the name suggested by a marketing person. Instead, back in 1929, "Texas" was chosen, because the state was known for its spicy food, and "Pete" was his son Harold's nickname.

... & More Sauces

Texas Pete was not the first sauce concocted by the Warner family. The country was about to enter the Great Depression when one of Sam Garner's sons, Thad, used his college money to buy a local restaurant. The restaurant served a barbecue sauce made by following a secret recipe, and although the restaurant didn't survive, the sauce did. The Garner family made it in the family kitchen, with Sam peddling it on the road throughout North Carolina. This was the start of the T. W. Garner Food Company that now offers a range of condiments, including sriracha, salsa, wing sauce, and mustard.

TABASCO IN THE TWENTY-FIRST CENTURY

More than 150 years after the first bottle, Tabasco sauce is still going strong, but now the mash is aged for up to three years in oak barrels, using distilled white vinegar. According to Paul McIlhenny, a fourth-generation descendant, "In the first 22 years of business we produced 350,000 bottles of Tabasco." Nowadays, the company produces twice that amount every day. McIlhenny's Tabasco is sold in more than 195 countries with labels in 36 different languages.

Appearing in 1870, Tabasco is the oldest hot sauce company still in business.

Did You Know?

The British Parliament tried to ban Tabasco sauce from the dining room in the House of Commons in 1932, when the "Buy British" theme was popular. However, due to the number of complaints, the ban was retracted so the hot sauce could once again spice things up in Parliament.

Army Rations

During World War II and the Korean War, Tabasco sauce traveled with the American soldiers while they fought abroad. When servicemen fought in the Vietnam War, they were given a free bottle on request. By the time the U.S. Army was sent to the Gulf War, every third "Meal, Ready to Eat," or MRE, came with a mini bottle of Tabasco. These mini bottles are now standard in many ration packs.

Royal Approval

Queen Elizabeth II awarded a Royal Warrant to the McIlhenny Company in 2009 in recognition of supplying goods. However, it seems that it wasn't only the Queen who enjoyed a little spice. The Queen Mother had her staff look for Tabasco sauce throughout London during World War II, at a time when there was a shortage.

> **"**
> *England has always been very loyal to us, consistently ranking among the top markets in international sales. This is indeed a proud moment in Tabasco history.*
> **"**

Paul McIlhenny, fourth-generation president and CEO of McIlhenny Company, on receiving the Royal Warrant

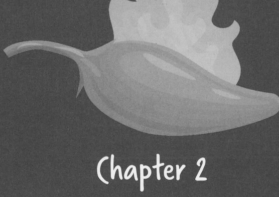

Chapter 2

Some Like It Hot

Hot sauce has been enjoyed for thousands of years, but what do we know about its most important ingredient—the chili?

Cultivated Chilies

It's impossible to tell exactly when people started turning chilies into spicy sauces, but there is archaeological evidence of humans using chilies as far back as 7,000 years ago in Peru. We know that at least 5,400 years ago, chilies were domesticated crops in Mexico, because there is evidence of the practice in Mexican cave dwellings.

WHO NEEDS MONEY?

Chilies were so important to the Peruvians that they could be used instead of money as a form of currency—not just in the distant past hundreds of years ago but as recently as the 1950s, when you could still use chilies to purchase items at the plaza in Cusco, Peru.

According to the USDA, on average 7.7 pounds (3.5 kg) of chilies were consumed by each person in the U.S. in 2017.

Speaking the Language

In the sense of meaning a hot pepper, the word
"chili" first appeared in the Spanish language in
1604; however, the Spaniards took the word from the
Nahuatl word *chil*. Nahuatl is the indigenous language
that was widely spoken by the Aztecs in Mexico before
the Spanish conquest in the sixteenth century.
There is, of course, also the South American country
called Chile, but the origins for its name is a story
for another time.

Chili Pepper or Chile . . .

Fast forward a few centuries, and there's been debate about whether the spelling of the hot pod should end in an "e" or an "i." The Association of Food Journalists recommends "chili" (plural, "chilies"), based on a style book by the Associated Press (AP) and Merriam-Webster's dictionary. However, the latter now gives "chile" as a variant spelling of chili.

... or Is It Chilli?

In the U.S., "chili" is used when the fresh pod has been transferred into another form, such as in chili powder, chili sauce, or a Mexican dish made with meat and hot peppers, such as chili con carne. However, in other countries, such as the U.K., Australia, and India, the preferred spelling is "chilli"—even for the peppers.

The Relatives

Bell peppers and chilies are members of the same nightshade plant family, Solanaceae, and among their other relatives are tomatoes, eggplant, and potatoes. However, chilies and bell peppers are not related to the *Piper nigrum* plant that provide us with peppercorns, which come from the pepper family, Piperaceae.

Did You Know?

The Anaheim chili gets its name from
a cannery that opened in 1900 in the
Californian city of the same name.
However, this particular chili, which is mild
and popular for stuffing, has two different
names in Mexico, where people use chili
verde to refer to the green version and
chili colorado when it's red.

Why Are Chilies Hot?

Chili plants have evolved by making their fruit (the peppers) seem to burn to stop mice and other mammals, including people, from eating them. However, birds are not affected by this trickery! Most animals have teeth that grind up the seeds and destroy them, which is why the plants evolved to prevent animals eating them, but birds are different. Birds eat the seeds whole, then disperse them when they poop, helping the plants to spread.

WHAT MAKES CHILIES HOT?

Chilies get their distinctive heat from a chemical compound called capsaicin (Kap-SAY-ih-sin), which creates a burning sensation on the tongue or skin.

However, this sensation isn't caused by being burned but by the body's pain response system. Capsaicin activates a protein called TRPV1, which is responsible for sensing heat and alerting the brain, which then sends a pain signal to the affected area. So, while you might burn your skin by grabbing a hot saucepan, you won't burn yourself by eating a hot pepper—the chili has simply tricked your brain into thinking it has!

Pain Relief

In small doses, chilies can help relieve pain. The TRPV1 protein (see page 49) that senses heat also floods pain-sensing nerves with calcium, which in turn has an effect on fatty substances called lipids, causing them to dip. When this happens, two other proteins that control how blood vessels constrict are affected and block signals of pain from being sent to the brain. This explains why rubbing creams that include capsaicin can be used to help relieve arthritis and other aches and pains.

"

When axi [chili] is taken moderately, it helps and comforts the stomacke for digestion: but if they take too much, it hath bad effects, for of its self it is very hote, fuming, and piercest greatly . . .

"

Father José de Acosta, Jesuit priest and naturalist

TAKE YOUR
MEDICINE

There were a number of medicinal uses for chilies
in the Americas before the arrival of the Spaniards.
They were used by the Mayans, for example, to treat
asthma, coughs, and sore throats, and in Columbia,
the Tukano people used them to relieve a hangover—
by pouring a mixture of chilies and water into their
nostrils! The Teeneks in Mexico rubbed it into wounds
to cure them of infection, but sometimes the pain was
severe enough to cause the "patient" to pass out. The
Aztecs used a drop or two to relieve toothache.

Take Your Punishment

It seems that chilies weren't used only to help people feel better, but also to feel worse. The Aztecs' daily way of life was described in the Mendocino Codex—a codex uses illustrations as a way of recording events. It shows a father punishing his son by making him inhale the smoke of chilies being roasted on a hearth, as well as a mother threatening to punish her daughter in the same way. This could be seen as an early version of pepper spray (see page 58).

Chilies Are Full of Goodness

As well as capsaicin, chilies have nutrients that are good for you. In fact, they have more vitamin C than oranges, with about 242 mg for every 100 g (3½ oz) compared to 53 mg for the same weight of an orange. Chilies also provide vitamin B6, iron, copper, and potassium.

Eat Chilies to Lose Weight

When eating something that contains capsaicin, it triggers the production of stress hormones, which is what makes someone sweat and causes skin to redden. These hormones are also part of the fight-or-flight response. To provide energy to deal with this mechanism, the body may need to convert its fat store to energy. Scientists are looking at how a capsaicin-based drug might help obese people to lose weight.

A Natural High

Some people have a sense of feeling more euphoric after eating chilies. This is because the brain secretes endorphins—the feel-good chemicals—to help counteract the sensation of burning. At the end of the sixteenth century, a Jesuit priest, Father José de Acosta, recorded, "the use thereof is prejudiciall to the health of young folks, chiefly to the soule, for that it provokes to lust."

Pepper Spray

In case you had been thinking that the pepper in pepper spray is from peppercorns, let's set the record straight. The ingredient in the pepper spray used for self-defense is capsaicin. The spray contains high enough levels of capsaicin to burn an attacker's eyes and throat: 2 million SHU (see page 60) in a pepper spray carried in a purse, but 5.3 million SHU if it is sprayed by the police.

Size
Matters

In general, the smaller the chili, the hotter it will be. This is because smaller chilies have more seeds and white membrane inside them than larger ones do, and it's the membrane that contains about 80 percent of the capsaicin that provides the heat. The world record holders tend to be under 2¾ inches (7 cm) long!

THE SCOVILLE SCALE

Wilbur Scoville created the Scoville Scale in 1912 by measuring the pungency levels in chilies by first grinding them up and diluting them in water until it could no longer be detected. The more water needed to dilute the pepper, the spicier the plant. A rating of zero Scoville heat units (SHU) represents the mildest bell pepper, a typical jalapeño pepper comes in at about 5,000 SHU, and superhot chilies above 2 million SHU.

SHU *for Everyday Chilies*

Listed here are the Scoville heat units for chilies that you can probably find in your local grocery store. If you're not sure how hot a hot sauce is, look for these on the label to give you an indication.

Pimento: 100–500 SHU

Shishito: 100–1,000 SHU

Paprika: 250–1,000 SHU

Anaheim: 500–2,500 SHU

Poblano: 1,000–2,000 SHU

Jalapeño: 2,500–8,000 SHU

Serrano: 10,000–25,000 SHU

Cayenne: 30,000–50,000 SHU

Thai (bird's-eye): 50,000–100,000 SHU

Piri piri: 50,000–100,000 SHU

Scotch bonnet: 100,000–325,000 SHU

Habanero: 150,000–350,000 SHU

Officially the Hottest Pepper

According to the Guinness World Records, Smokin' Ed's Carolina Reaper wins the competition of being the world's hottest chili, which was rated at an average of 1,641,183 SHU when tests were carried out at Winthrop University, South Carolina, in 2017. The chili was first released by Ed Currie of the PuckerButt Pepper Company in 2013 and has since topped its own world record by reaching 2,200,000 SHU. (As a comparison, a hot habanero might reach 500,000 SHU.)

Unofficial Hottest Peppers

PuckerButt Pepper Company has reportedly come up with an even hotter chili—the Pepper X, at 3.18 million SHU. Dragon's Breath, originally developed in the U.K., is another chili rumored to be hotter than the Carolina Reaper, at 2.48 million SHU. Neither have yet been recognized by Guinness World Records.

Top 10 Hottest Chilies

Gone are the days when the ghost pepper, or bhut jolokia, was the world record holder for the hottest chili in 2006, at 1,001,304 SHU. As of December 2020, it has dropped to 21st place in the list of the world's hottest chilies.

1. **Carolina Reaper:** 2,200,000 SHU (beating its own Guinness World Record)
2. **Trinidad Moruga Scorpion:** 2,009,231 SHU
3. **Chocolate Bhutlah:** 2,000,000 SHU
4. **7 Pot Douglah:** 1,853,936 SHU*
5. **Chocolate 7 Pot:** 923,000–1,850,000 SHU*
6. **Dorset Naga:** 1,000,000–1,500,000 SHU
7. **Naga Morich:** 1,000,000–1,500,000 SHU
8. **7 Pot Primo:** 1,473,480 SHU*
9. **Trinidad Scorpion Butch T:** 1,463,700 SHU
10. **Komodo Dragon:** 1,400,000 SHU

Note: The inclusion of "7 pot" in the name indicates that one chili can be used to spice seven pots of food.

Reaping a New Record

After two previous attempts in October 2016, the PuckerButt Pepper Company found a winner for their challenge: to eat the most Carolina Reaper chilies in a minute. At the Arizona Hot Sauce Expo, Greg Foster from Irvine, California, managed to eat 120 grams of the pepper company's hot peppers in 60 seconds, beating the previous record holder by one gram.

> ❝
> *Eating even one Carolina Reaper pepper challenges the most daring of Pepperheads.*
> ❞

Ed Currie, founder and president of PuckerButt Pepper Company

Longest Habanero Kiss

According to Guinness World Records, the longest habanero kiss, in which Lance Michael Rich and Matthew Clint Burnham held a kiss after eating habanero chilies, lasted for 3 minutes 36.86 seconds, on May 8, 2021, in Shreveport, Louisiana. The habanero may not be the hottest chili, but it is fiery, at between 100,000 and 350,000 SHU.

Can Eating Superhot Chilies Cause Death?

The short answer is no, although there have been false claims of superhot chilies leading to anaphylactic shock or death. Although chilies cannot actually burn or tear body parts (see page 49), they can cause nausea, vomiting, and stomach pain, and the acids from vomiting can cause problems. However, you can overdose on capsaicin—if you eat more than 3 pounds (1.36 kg) of superhot chilies, which is highly unlikely. If you have certain medical conditions, it's probably better to forego the Carolina Reaper.

When It's Too Hot!

Why is it that water doesn't help to cool down your tongue after eating a chili or hot sauce that's too hot? It's because capsaicin is not soluble in water, so water doesn't do a good job of diluting it. You'll need something fatty to destroy the bond between capsaicin and the pain receptors in your tongue, which is why you should reach for a drink or food with the protein casein, such as milk, yogurt, or ice cream.

Chapter 3

Hot Sauces from Distant Places

The New World doesn't have a monopoly on the chili. It's enjoyed by millions of people around the world and in many international cuisines.

Why Are Chilies Also Called Peppers?

One story goes that Christopher Columbus brought chilies back with him from America to Europe in 1493 to help preserve meats over the long voyage across the Atlantic Ocean. The Europeans didn't recognize the chili as anything they knew, but thinking that they were similar to black pepper, they gave them the same name.

It's Not Caucasian Pepper

Peter Martyr d'Anghiera (1455–1526), referring to Christopher Columbus's introduction of chili to Spain in 1493, wrote that it was

"... a pepper more pungent than that from the Caucasus."

He also wrote:

"Something may be said about the pepper gathered in the islands and on the continent ... but it is not pepper, though it has the same strength and the flavor, and is just as much esteemed. The natives call it axi."

Across the Atlantic

Through their sixteenth-century voyages to the West Indies, Mexico, Peru, and Chile, the Spanish were introduced to different types of chilies, which they took back with them to Spain. Unlike tomatoes and potatoes, Europeans were more willing to try chilies, perhaps because of their mistaken identity of being pepper. Chilies reached England in 1548 and Central Europe about 1585.

ITALIAN CHILIES

From Spain, the chili was introduced to Italy in 1526, where it began to be cultivated. Sicilians use them processed into a paste, and it is believed that the spicy pizza diavolo (*diavolo* meaning "devil") has been popular in Naples since the Baroque period. Pietro Andrea Mattioli, a Renaissance physician and botanist, described the "peperoncini" for the first time in a book in 1568, in which he mentioned that it was much hotter than chilies imported from Asia. Today, peperoncini, aka Tuscan peppers or sweet Italian peppers, are considered sweet and mild; they are often pickled.

Portuguese Traders

Although it may seem that the Spanish were responsible for introducing chilies to Europe and elsewhere, the Portuguese were actually more influential through their well-established trade routes. This can be established by the species of chili; the Portuguese transported the *Capsicum annuum* var. *annuum* species during their travels, while Columbus brought the *Capsicum chinense* pepper to Spain.

Brazilian Chilies Reach Africa

When trying to find a route to "the Indies" in 1500, the Portuguese came across chilies in Brazil, known locally as *quijà* or *quiya*. Along with corn, pineapple, and manioc, they took these foodstuffs by ship to Africa, along the coasts of the Gulf of Guinea, Mozambique, and Angola, where they were quickly incorporated into the local dishes.

Peri Peri

As the story goes, Portuguese explorers in Mozambique used African bird's-eye chilies to make a marinade with garlic, red wine vinegar, paprika, and other ingredients, making the first peri peri. The name is derived from the Swahili *piri piri*, which means "pepper pepper." The Portuguese took the sauce with them when they traveled to other Portuguese territories.

Elephant Repellent

It's unlikely that you live anywhere that you might have to keep elephants away. However, if you do, here's a trick that works in parts of Africa—use chilies to keep elephants out of your crops. Elephants hate the smell of chilies!

BACK TO
AMERICA

Although chilies had made their way from Central and South America to some regions in the U.S., chilies only became firmly established in the nation when slaves were transported from the West Indies and West Africa, places where chilies were established in local cuisines.

Europe to Asia

From the 1540s onward, the Portuguese introduced chilies along the Silk Road, from Afghanistan to Samarkand, and from Nepal to China. In India, where cooks were already using spices like black pepper and ginger, people quickly welcomed chilies, according to an early sixteenth-century report from a Portuguese official in India. In 1542, Portuguese missionaries brought the chili to Japan, from where it traveled to Korea.

Chilies Arrive in the Middle East

Andalusian Muslims and Jews migrated to Tunisia in the northern-most region in Africa, after being expelled from Spain by the Spanish Christians in the late sixteenth century. They brought with them chilies, which would eventually become an integral part of the Tunisian cuisine and an essential ingredient for harissa.

Harissa

Tunisia is the home of harissa, a hot sauce or paste made from a base of red baklouti chilies that is seasoned with cumin and coriander. The name comes from the Arabic verb *harasa*, which means "to pound" or "break into pieces." The hot sauce is popular throughout the Maghreb, including a version made with rose petals. The flavor varies depending on the country, region, and even neighborhood. In Tunisia, it is considered the country's main condiment. Libyans enjoy harissa with fast food, pizza, and egg sandwiches.

"

When a meal is spicy enough to make your sinus runny, the food is complimented for cleaning out the airways.

"

Huda Biuk, *Libyan Post* culture columnist,
commenting on harissa

Fit for Kings

The Turks first introduced the chili to Hungary in 1570. Because it was a rare plant at the time, only the aristocracy could afford to enjoy the pungent peppers. However, as it became more common, it eventually became part of the Hungarian cuisine.
The name "paprika" was first coined by the Hungarians in 1724.

A quarter of the world's population —nearly 2 billion people—eat chilies every day!

By Another Name

Here are some other names for chili that you might see on menus or labels:

Boliva: **Aji**

Chile: **Aji**

China: **Laoganma**

Colombia: **Aji**

Ecuador: **Aji**

Egypt: **Shatta**

Ethiopia: **Awaze**

Ghana: **Shito**

Hungary: **Eros pista**

Indonesia: **Sambal**

Korea: **Gochujang**

North Africa: **Harissa**

Peru: **Aji**

Portugal: **Peri peri**

Syria: **Muhammara**

Thailand: **Nam phrik**

Vietnam: **Sriracha**

The Middle Eastern Shatta

Although it's found throughout the Levant, hence also being known as Levantine hot sauce or Middle Eastern hot sauce, shatta is especially appreciated in Egypt and Palestine—its origins are in Gaza. This hot sauce has the consistency of a paste, and while commercial jarred versions are usually made with 50 percent vinegar to prolong storage, homemade types can include both olive oil and vinegar. Unlike other hot sauces, fresh chilies are used in making shatta.

The Middle Eastern Zhug

Whether you call it zhug, shoug, schug, or Yemenite hot sauce, this is a usually bright green Israeli hot sauce made with serrano chilies along with oil, fresh herbs, and garlic—the green color is traditionally from cilantro leaves, though a mixture of half cilantro and half parsley is often used today. Red versions use red chilies, and a brown version includes tomatoes. It is a milder sauce than its spicier neighbor, shatta.

Did You Know?

Before refrigeration, chilies could be used to help keep food safe. In warm weather, microbes can multiply on food, making them unsafe to eat without getting sick. The capsaicin and other chemicals in chilies can slow down or stop microbial growth. This might be why spicy foods seem to be more popular in hot countries, such as India and Mexico. At first, people ate chilies because they liked them, but they also survived longer and raised healthier families, leading to future generations of peoples who inherited a love for spices.

CHINESE
CHILI SAUCE

The Chinese version of hot sauce—which is more often referred to as a chili sauce—comes in a paste form, and many varieties involve using it with a pickling solution during the cooking process. They vary based on the region: Guilin chili sauce from the southern Chinese city, for example, is made with fermented soybeans. Although it is not a chili sauce, chili oil, in which chilies are steeped in oil, is also popular in China.

Healthy Life

According to a 2015 study, researchers following half a million Chinese adults over seven years discovered that those who ate spicy food six or seven days a week were 14 percent less likely to die early. If you visit a restaurant in China, you will probably find a chili sauce on the table.

The Godmother of Chili Sauce

One of the most popular of Chinese chili sauces is Laoganma, and in China it is sometimes considered the "godmother of all lazy Chinese foodies." It was first served in 1996 in a small shop selling noodles by Tao Huabi, who then went on to mass produce her popular sauce. Today it is now sold outside of China in Asian markets and grocery stores.

Longest Chili String

According to the Guinness World Records, 2,533 people participated in making the world's longest string of chilies on October 11, 2008. They used 29,037 red chilies to make a string that measured 4,576 feet 9 inches (1,395 m) long. The event took place in Suncheon City, South Korea (Republic of Korea).

SUPERHOT CHILIES, U.K. STYLE

It may seem unlikely, but two of the world's hottest chilies were first grown in the U.K.: the Naga Viper chili (with 1,382,11 SHU) and the Infinity chili (with 1,067,2868 SHU). This also means that there are some particularly hot, hot sauces being served in that country, too, where Indian and Bangladeshi immigrants introduced curries.

Have a Chili with your Meal

Although the Naga chili, or Naga Morich, is sometimes cooked in a dish in Bangladesh, it is more often consumed raw, in an underripe green stage, alongside other foods. The fruit is offered at the table whole, where a piece is broken off and mixed with cooked rice or other accompaniments on a plate. The Naga Morich is appreciated in Bangladesh for its aroma of apricots and bubblegum.

The capsaicin in chilies helped scientists understand how the body converts stimuli into pain, when they used it in experiments and discovered receptors for temperature and touch. For their research, David Julius and Ardem Patapoutian were jointly awarded the Nobel Prize in Physiology or Medicine in 2021. There is hope that their research will lead to breakthroughs in pain relief.

The hot sauce market is on fire. The global market was valued at $4.31 billion in 2020—and it is predicted to increase by 5.3 percent to a value of $5.8 billion in 2026.

Hot Sauce
Vietnamese Style

One of the most popular hot sauces in Vietnam
is made by Tran Van Can, aka Ms. Van, who uses
elephant tusk chilies and follows a 150-year-old recipe
passed down her family, originally of Chinese descent.
She started off giving away her Hoi An sauce to
relatives, but soon people were clamoring to buy it.

Sriracha
Thai Style

The popular sweet hot sauce used in Thailand is named for the town of Si Racha, a district known for its chilies and seafood. A Thai woman called Thanom Chakkapak is thought to have first made it in 1949, when she bottled it as Sriraja Panich, but it's unclear if this is the original sauce. Regardless, Sriraja Panich is now one of the country's favorites, and following the Thai palate, it has layers of sweet, sour, and salt. It is sweeter and thinner than the popular American version (see page 108).

Top 10 Hot Sauces

According to a survey taken in 2014, the following are the world's top 10 favorite hot sauces. Have a taste test to see which one you prefer.

1. **Huy Fong Sriracha,** Thai-style hot sauce made in California
2. **Cholula,** a Mexican hot sauce
3. **Crystal,** one of the Louisiana-style hot sauces
4. **Frank's RedHot,** another Louisiana-style hot sauce
5. **Huy Fong Chili Garlic,** a thick, garlicky hot sauce
6. **Louisiana Hot Sauce Original,** the name says it all
7. **Tapatío,** a sweet, garlicky hot sauce great for Bloody Marys
8. **Tabasco,** the classic made by the McIlhenny family
9. **Texas Pete,** a mild hot sauce that's become an American staple
10. **Valentina Salsa Picante,** a sweet-and-sour Mexican hot sauce with a citrusy tang

Chapter 4

A Love Affair with Hot Sauce

Discover the incredible range of spicy condiments available and why they've proven to be so popular in the Americas and beyond.

An Explosion of Sauces

There's an astounding number of hot sauces available, from superhot hot sauces to ones specifically for serving with chicken wings, from mass market sauces to limited editions. As of June 2022, Hot Sauce Fever, a database on the Internet, listed almost 600 different hot sauces. Hot Sauce Survey also provides hot sauce lovers with an array of information on various products.

"

... there's lots and lots of kinds of hot sauces, and not so many kinds of mustard. Not because it's hard to make interesting mustard—you could make interesting mustard—but people don't, because no one's obsessed with it, and thus no one tells their friends.

"

Seth Godin, author

According to a Instacart-Harris Poll survey, 74 percent of Americans like to put hot sauce on their food— and 45 percent of those said they do so once a week or more.

How to Become a Pepperhead

For a newbie, always start with a mild sauce, which will concentrate on flavor rather than heat. Add a few drops to your food while cooking, or you can even add a little sriracha to your mayonnaise to spread on a sandwich. Gradually switch to a hotter sauce, but always taste before drizzling to avoid ruining your food. Dipping the tines of a fork into the sauce is a good way to get a small dose.

Sriracha!

One of America's favorite hot sauces, Huy Fong's sriracha sauce, had humble beginnings. David Tran, a Chinese immigrant from Vietnam, first sold his version of the sweet-and-spicy Thai-style sriracha sauce in 1980 from a van parked in Los Angeles. It would take almost another three decades before his sriracha finally hit the shelves in Walmart in 2003. Even so, many people are still pronouncing it wrong—it should be pronounced see-rotch-a!

Rooster Sauce

Huy Fong's sriracha is also known as the rooster sauce, because of the rooster that features on the bright red bottle's label. David Tran, the sauce's creator, was born in 1945, the year of the rooster in the Chinese zodiac. Along with the green cap, the rooster logo is trademarked, but not the name "sriracha."

L.A. Hit

Taptío hot sauce was first sold in 5-ounce (150-g) bottles in 1971 when Jose-Luis Saavedra Sr. began producing it in a 750-foot-square (70-m^2) building in East Los Angeles. This West Coast sauce gets its flavor from the habanero chili and is particularly popular among Mexican Americans. After a collaboration in 2011, Frito-Lay began producing Taptío-flavored tortilla chips.

Hot Sauce, Mexican Style

Chipotle are considered the favorite chilies for making hot sauce in Mexico. Unlike the U.S.'s obsession with heat, Mexicans prefer to make sauces that concentrate more on the chili's flavor. However, the American trend for heat may be receding in the wake of the new wave of craft hot sauces that are being developed with fresh ingredients and flavor in mind.

Cholula

Arbol and piquin chilies, along with regional spices, go into making this popular hot sauce from Mexico. Pronounced "choe-loo-la," the hot sauce is named for the city of Cholula, which happens to be the oldest still-inhabited town in Central America, going back 2,500 years. A bottle of Cholula can be picked out by its distinctive wooden cap, which is color-coded to match each flavor.

Caribbean Chilies

The countries in the Caribbean make their hot pepper sauces from habanero chilies and Scotch bonnet chilies, with the latter making a particularly potent hot sauce. The small round Scotch bonnet looks somewhat like the pom-pom on the Scottish hat.

> **"**
>
> *I'm a big fan of Caribbean food, Spanish food, Dominican food—like rice and beans. Hot sauce just adds a different layer of boom to the food, you feel me?*
>
> **"**

Theophilus London, singer

The Original Pickapeppa

Fondly known as Jamaican ketchup, this sweet, sour, and mildy spicy brand is flavored with cane sugar, cloves, raisins, and pepper. It was founded in 1921, with its spicier Scotch bonnet version appearing later. A reputed favorite of model Naomi Campbell, one traditional use is to pour it over cream cheese and serve it as a dip.

Did You Know?

Because hot sauces combine vinegar with chilies, they have an impressive shelf life. An unopened bottle can last for years, as long as the seal hasn't been broken. Once the bottle is opened, it can be safe to use for up to six months when kept at room temperature; however, if you store that same bottle in the refrigerator, you can expect it to last for up to five years—but it will probably be used up long before then.

The First Buffalo Chicken Wings

Ever wondered how Buffalo chicken wings got that name? The town of Buffalo, in upstate New York, is where Frank's RedHot sauce and butter were first used in 1934 to season chicken wings at the Anchor Bar & Grill. Nowadays, the same seasonings can be used for cauliflower so even vegans can enjoy this wonderful combination of ingredients.

The First Bloody Mary

Version No. 1

There are a few tales relating to the first time a Bloody Mary was concocted. One version claims that the French bartender Fernand Petiot invented it in 1921 at the New York Bar in Paris by adding Tabasco sauce to a tomato-based cocktail. However, in 1964, Petiot told the *New Yorker* magazine that he created the cocktail in 1934 in the King Cole Room in the St. Regis Hotel in New York City.

The First Bloody Mary

Version No. 2

There is another story that claims the Broadway actor George Jessel invented the Bloody Mary in Palm Beach, Florida, in 1927, when trying to mask the smell of vodka. He claimed that he offered it to Mary Brown Warburton, but it spilled down the front of her white evening dress. She laughed it off, saying, "Now you can call me Bloody Mary, George!"

In the U.S. alone, hot sauce is a $1.5 billion industry, which is larger than the combined sales of all the other condiments.

Top 10 Hottest Hot Sauces

1. **Mad Dog 357 No. 9 Plutonium:** 9 million SHU
2. **The Source Hot Sauce:** 7.1 million SHU
3. **The End Hot Sauce:** 6 million SHU
4. **Get Bitten Black Mamba 6 Hot Sauce:** 6 million SHU
5. **Bumblef**ked Hot Sauce:** 6 million SHU
6. **Mad Dog 357 Pepper Extract:** 5 million SHU
7. **Meet Your Maker Death Sauce:** 5 million SHU
8. **Mad Dog 44 Magnum:** 4 million SHU
9. **Z Nothing Beyond Extremely Hot Sauce:** unknown
10. **Hottest Sauce in the Universe 2nd Dimension:** 3.5 million SHU

> **"**
> *No, our motto is
> 'Everything tastes better with
> hot sauce.'*
> **"**

Sherrilyn Kenyon, *Bad Moon Rising* (2009)

National
Hot Sauce Day is
celebrated each year
in the U.S. on
January 22.

Hot Ones

The first season of the infamous television series *Hot Ones* was first aired on YouTube in 2015. It features celebrities being interviewed while eating increasingly spicy chicken wings. Here's a list of the hot sauces that appeared in the first season.

1. Texas Pete Original
2. Cholula Original Hot Sauce
3. El Yucateco Caribbean Hot Sauce
4. Lottie's Traditional Barbados Yellow Pepper Sauce
5. Pain Is Good Louisiana Style
6. Pain 100% Hot Sauce
7. Blair's Original Death Sauce
8. Dave's Gourmet Temporary Insanity Hot Sauce
9. Dave's Gourmet Insanity Hot Sauce
10. Mad Dog 357 Hot Sauce

Organize Your Own Hot Sauce Party

1. Choose a range of hot sauces from mild to hot, hot, hot.
2. Line them up for your guests, from mildest to hottest. In case they get swapped, label them with numbers.
3. Make chicken wings or order them from a takeout. Plan on 8 to 10 wings per person.
4. Make sure you have plenty of milk or ice cream on standby, and napkins.
5. Starting with the mildest, add some sauce to a chicken wing for each guest, and see who can continue to the strongest sauce.

Source: goodfoodpittsburgh.com

How to Remove a Hot Sauce Stain from a Carpet

If a guest got carried away with a hot sauce challenge and spilled, first blot up (not rub) the spill with clean paper towels, working from the outside edge in to the center. Dilute the stain with a few drops of water and blot again with clean paper towels, then mix one part nonbleach laundry detergent with four parts warm water (or one part vinegar and one part water), apply it to the stain, and let sit for 3 minutes before using a clean cloth to blot it up. Repeat until no longer visible. Rinse with plain water.

How to Remove a Hot Sauce Stain from Clothes

Act quickly. First, remove any solids with the edge of a spoon, then hold the front and back of the stained area under cold running water for at least a minute (hot water will set a stain). Gently scrub the stain with dishwashing liquid or a mixture of vinegar and water. If it remains, let soak for 30 minutes and scrub a second time. Wash in the washing machine, using a laundry stain remover if the stain is still visible—and don't use hot water.

Hot Sauce and Chili Festivals

There are various festivals around the U.S. each year celebrating hot sauces and chilies.

1. NYC Hot Sauce Expo, Brooklyn, New York

2. National Buffalo Wing Festival, Buffalo, New York

3. National Fiery Foods Show, Albuquerque, New Mexico

4. ZestFest, Irving, Texas

5. *Austin Chronicle* Hot Sauce Festival, Austin, Texas

6. California Hot Sauce Expo, Anaheim, California

7. I Like it Hot Festival, Largo, Florida

8. Hop Sauce Festival, Long Beach Island, New Jersey

9. Pueblo Chilies and Frijoles Festival, Pueblo, Colorado

10. Pinellas Pepper Fest, Pinellas Park, Florida

King of the Collectors

Vic Clinco has been collecting bottles of hot sauce for more than 20 years and has over 8,600 sealed bottles on display in his living room. They vary from those found in a Hispanic grocery store for just 79 cents to a whopping $350 for a reserve bottle.

A Collector's Treasure

Only 499 bottles have been made of the infamous Blair's Reserve Caldera. The bottle has a gold-covered skull on its cap and inside the nearly 1-foot (25-cm) tall bottle are three layers of capsaicin oils, each one hotter than the other. In 2018 it was reported that one was selling for $2,700.

Chapter 5

Homegrown and Homemade

Grow your own chilies and make your own homemade artisan sauces, as flavorful and fiery as you like.

Sowing Seeds Indoors

Even if you want to grow chilies outdoors, start them indoors at least 8 weeks before the last predicted frost. Plant two seeds (in case one doesn't sprout) in 1½ to 2-inch (4 to 5-cm) pots filled with seed-starting soil, top with a thin layer of the soil, and water. See the packet directions for the best planting depth. Keep the seeds at 85°F (29.4°C).

Caring for Seedlings

Keep the soil moist but not soggy. Wilting can be a sign of too much or too little water. Use warm water and check the soil with a finger to determine if it feels dry. After about 10 days, you should see the seedlings sprout. When two pairs of leaves appear, you can move the seedlings into larger pots filled with a growing medium. If two seeds grow, use a pair of scissors to snip off the weaker plant at the base, after the plants settle.

Moving Plants Outdoors

Once the soil temperature outdoors is above 60°F (15.5°C), you can plant the chilies outside, leaving 12 to 18 inches (30–45 cm) between plants. However, first "harden them off" by placing the plants outdoors in the daytime and bringing them in at night. About a week beforehand, reduce the amount of watering and stop fertilizing.

Did You Know?

Chilies grow wild only in the New World and the fruit looks more like berries. Along with hybridization, over thousands of years of breeding, there are now more than 50,000 chili pepper cultivars, mostly from only five species: *Capsicum annuum*, *Capsicum chinense*, *Capsicum frutescens*, *Capsicum baccatum*, and *Capsicum pubescens*.

Indoor Plants

Chilies can be grown successfully indoors in flowerpots on sunny windowsills. You don't have to start growing the plants from seeds. Visit a garden center to choose some chili plants, then transfer them to attractive flowerpots with drainage holes and saucers.

Record-Breaking Chilies

The heaviest chili, according to Guinness World Records, was grown by Paul Davies in Halesowen, U.K. The pepper weighed 16.2 ounces (460 grams) on September 7, 2020.

The longest chili, a cayenne pepper that was grown by Jürg Wiesli of Switzerland, measured 19.8 inches (505 mm) long from the "shoulder," where it is thickest, to the tip.

In the U.S., 4.7 million pounds of chilies were grown on 11,500 acres in 2020, with a value of $100 million.

Pick a Pepper

When you want to harvest a chili or two, cut them off the stem while the pod is still firm. You can harvest chilies while still green, but the redder the chilies, the hotter they will be. At the end of the growing season, harvest all the chilies and freeze the ones you can't use in a ziplock bag. Chop the chilies while still frozen to add to your dishes.

Handle with Care

Always protect your hands with a pair of disposable gloves, and never rub your eyes after handling. The capsaicin in the chilies can burn your skin, and the effect lasts for hours, so can affect you long after you've handled them. Be cautious when handling knives and cutting boards used to prepare chilies in the kitchen, too. You've been warned!

Did You Know?

Even when the type of chili is the same, the peppers from two plants may not be alike. Their heat can vary due to variations in the soil and climate conditions; for example, a plant grown in one country can produce peppers different than those grown in another. This is true for other fruit and vegetables—just think about wines grown from the same type of grapes but in different countries.

Chili Ristras

In New Mexico, strings of red chilies are hung from fences or patios for drying. These *ristras* (Spanish for "string") are said to bring good health and good luck. To make your own, thread a long piece of strong string through a sewing needle and knot the end. Thread clean, dry chilies onto the string, pushing the needle into the thickest part of each stem.
Tie a loop on the end and rotate the chilies to form a spiral to expose them to air. Hang to dry for 3 to 4 weeks before using.

In New Mexico, where chilies are an essential ingredient for Mexican and Southwestern food, people consume more chilies per capita than any other state in the country.

New Mexico Hot Sauce

This recipe is ideal for using dry chilies from your homemade *ristra* (see page 144). You can freeze any leftover puree.

    12 to 14 large dry red chilies
    1 cup (250 ml) water
    1 clove garlic, minced
    ½ teaspoon salt
    2 tablespoons vegetable oil
    ½ teaspoon crushed dry oregano leaves

Wash the pods well in warm water, then let soak for 30 minutes to 1 hour until rehydrated. Put the pods with a little water into a blender or food processor, then blend to a puree. Press the puree through a sieve to remove any tiny pieces.

In a saucepan, add 1 cup (250 ml) of the puree with the water, garlic, salt, and vegetable oil and simmer for 10 minutes. Add the oregano and simmer for 5 to 7 minutes.

Seeding Chilies

Cookbooks recommend removing the seeds and membranes or veins from a chili—basically it's placenta—if you prefer less heat. This is because capsaicin is produced at the stem end. However, if you like your dishes spicy, don't de-seed the chilies. A whole chili can be added to dishes for extra spice, but remove it before serving.

Easy Louisiana Hot Sauce

Chilies are fermented in traditional Louisiana-style hot sauces, but here's a quick version.

1 pound (450 g) fresh red chilies, such as tabasco, stems removed but not seeded
2 cups (500 ml) distilled white vinegar
1 tablespoon salt

Add the chilies, vinegar, and salt to a large saucepan over high heat and bring to a simmer. Reduce the heat to medium and simmer for 5 minutes, until the chilies are soft.

Transfer to a blender and blend until smooth. Strain to remove the seeds. Let rest at room temperature, then refrigerate for at least 30 minutes before use.

Classic Louisiana Hot Sauce

The fermentation process produces a mellower, more developed flavor. You may also like to use other chilies, such as long cayennes, red jalapeños, or even superhots.

1 pound (450 g) tabasco chilies, chopped
4 cups (950 ml) unchlorinated water
3 tablespoons salt
¾ cup (175 ml) white distilled vinegar

Pack the chilies into a clean screw-top jar until 1 inch (2.5 cm) from the top. Mix the water with the salt, then pour over the chilies until covered. Secure the lid.

Place the jar in a dark, cool place for 1 to 2 weeks. Check daily to make sure the chilies remain submerged. The chilies will ferment and produce gases; unscrew the lid to let the gases escape as needed.

When the fermentation slows down, and the solution turns cloudy, pour the chilies and solution into a saucepan with the vinegar. Bring to a boil, reduce the heat, and simmer for 15 minutes. Let cool, then blend until smooth. Strain, then store in the refrigerator.

Variations for Hot Sauces

Try varying hot sauce recipes by getting creative and playing around with the portions and ingredients:

- Change the chili—try jalapeño, serrano, cayenne, or any other you like.
- Use white wine vinegar for a mellow flavor, or rice vinegar if you prefer mellow and sweet. For a fruity flavor, try red wine vinegar, but use apple cider vinegar if you want fruity and sweet. For a strong flavor, choose malt or balsamic vinegar.
- Try adding fruit, such as chopped pineapple or mango.
- Add herbs, such as chopped fresh cilantro, basil, or parsley, or dried oregano or thyme.

Lady Marmalade Style

Patti LaBelle, who once said "Hot flavors always fascinated me," has taken her love of the hot stuff to the next level. She has her own line of hot sauces that are formulated to be more about flavor than heat. They include Hot Flash, which has a nice kick but doesn't burn, and Smoked Habenero, which works well with wings.

Hot Sauce Bottles and Equipment

If you plan to make only a small amount of hot sauce that will be used quickly, you can reuse an old hot sauce bottle as long as you clean it thoroughly, store the sauce in the refrigerator, and use it within a couple of weeks. However, if you're getting serious about making hot sauce, you might prefer to purchase hot sauce bottles—the 5-ounce woozy bottle is the most popular. If you don't have a small funnel in your kitchen already, you'll need to get one to help transfer the sauce to the bottle.

> **"**
>
> *I have a zillion bottles of hot sauce . . . The whole right side of my fridge is filled with hot sauce.*
>
> **"**

Lisa Ling, journalist and television personality

Piri Piri Sauce

Use this sauce to flavor chicken legs or wings for a real treat.

  1 pound (450 g) African bird's-eye or other hot red chilies, chopped
  4 cloves garlic, chopped
  1 teaspoon paprika
  ½ cup (20 g) chopped fresh cilantro
  ¼ cup (10 g) chopped fresh basil
  ½ cup (125 ml) vegetable oil
  Juice from 1 lemon
  Salt, to taste

Add all the ingredients to a blender or food processor and blend to form a smooth sauce. Strain or leave chunky, as you prefer.

Caribbean Hot Sauce

Each island has its own recipes, but here's a basic recipe to adapt to your preference.

1 pound (450 g) Scotch bonnet chilies, stems removed
1 tablespoon kosher salt
½ to 1 cup (125–250 ml) distilled white vinegar

Add the chilies and salt to a food processor, then pulse until the chilies are finely minced, scraping down the sides occasionally.

With the motor still running, pour in just enough vinegar to moisten the chilies and give the consistency of a thick sauce. Store in clean, airtight jars for 5 days to let the flavors develop.

Mango-Habanero Hot Sauce

Only a drop or two will add spice and fruitiness to seafood.

    1–2 tablespoons vegetable oil
    1 onion, coarsely chopped
    2 cloves garlic, whole
    6 habanero chilies, stems removed
    1 cup (165 g) chopped mango
    1-inch (2.5-cm) piece fresh ginger, peeled
    ¾ cup (175 ml) distilled white vinegar
    ½ cup (125 ml) water
    ½ teaspoon salt

Heat the oil in a skillet over medium heat, add the onion and whole garlic, and sauté for 5 minutes, then add the chilies, mango, ginger, vinegar, water, and salt. Let simmer for about 5 minutes. Transfer to a blender and blend until smooth.

ROCK YOUR WORLD

The lead guitarist for Aerosmith may have been
playing guitar for decades, but he's also started his
own hot sauce business. Boneyard Brew is made with
habaneros, onions, and garlic. Other sauces have also
been added to his Rock Your World line, including a
classic BBQ sauce and Mango Peach Tango.

Chipotle Hot Sauce

This smoky hot sauce will be thick enough to cling to tacos or potatoes.

  1 tablespoon vegetable oil
  ¼ small onion
  1 clove garlic, minced
  6 to 8 canned chipotles in adobo sauce, seeds removed
  ⅓ cup (75 ml) distilled white vinegar
  ⅓ cup (75 ml) water
  Juice of ½ orange
  ¾ teaspoon Mexican oregano
  ¼ teaspoon cumin
  Salt, to taste

Heat the oil in a skillet over medium heat, add the onion and garlic, and sauté for 5 minutes until browned. Transfer to a blender with the remaining ingredients and blend until smooth. Taste and adjust seasoning.

Aji Hot Sauce

This Peruvian-style sweet hot sauce is wonderful as a topping for sandwiches, tacos, or grilled meat. The color depends on the chilies chosen; add in vinegar to make a more traditional sauce.

    1 pound (450 g) cachucha or cayenne, and/or serrano chilies
    1 medium red onion, halved
    4 cloves garlic
    2 tablespoons honey
    1 tablespoon brown sugar
    1 teaspoon salt
    ¼ cup (60 ml) water

Put the chilies, onion, and garlic in a large saucepan, cover with water, and bring to a boil. Reduce the heat and simmer for 20 minutes, until the vegetables are soft. Drain.

Transfer the ingredients to a blender and blend to a thick paste. Add the honey, sugar, salt, and water, then blend until it becomes a homogenous mixture. Strain for a smooth sauce or leave chunky.

> **"**
>
> *I love hot sauce. It can't be hot enough for me.*
>
> **"**

Cheryl Hines, actress and director

Garlic-Chili Sauce

A red sriracha-style condiment that is great with noodles or chicken wings.

    8 ounces (225 g) red jalapeño chilies
    2 heads garlic
    1 teaspoon salt
    1 teaspoon sugar
    ⅓ cup (75 ml) distilled white vinegar
    1 tablespoon water
    1 teaspoon cornstarch mixed with 1 teaspoon water

Combine all the ingredients, except the cornstarch mixture, in a blender on medium speed until chunky. Remove one-quarter of the chunky mixture and reserve.

Liquify the remaining mixture on high speed, then strain, keeping the juices. Mix the strained juice with the reserved chunky mixture in a saucepan. Heat over medium-high heat, add the cornstarch mixture, and bring to a boil. Remove from the heat and let cool.

Sweet Chili Sauce

A Chinese-style condiment that is perfect for noodles, stir-fries, and pork dishes.

½ cup (125 ml) rice vinegar
½ cup (125 ml) water
½ cup (100 ml) granulated sugar
2 tablespoons Shaoxing wine
1 tablespoon soy sauce
3 bird's-eye chilies, seeded and minced
6 cloves garlic, minced
2 slices fresh ginger, minced
2 teaspoons cornstarch mixed with 3 tablespoon water

Add all the ingredients, except the cornstarch mixture, to a saucepan over medium-high heat. Stirring occasionally, bring to a boil. Reduce to medium heat and simmer for 5 minutes.

Reduce the heat to medium-low, add the cornstarch mixture, and stir for 1 minute; add a little water if too thick. Let cool.

Zhug

This Yemenite favorite goes well with fish and meat, and it can be used as a dip, sandwich topping, or even a barbecue sauce.

    20 serrano chilies, stems removed
    1 cup (25 g) fresh parsley leaves
    1 cup (25 g) fresh cilantro leaves
    4 cloves garlic
    1 tablespoon kosher salt
    1 tablespoon ground coriander
    1 tablespoon ground cardamom
    2 tablespoons lemon juice
    1 cup (250 ml) olive oil

In a food processor, add the chilies, parsley, cilantro, garlic, salt, coriander, cardamom, and lemon juice. Pulse until the ingredients form a coarse paste.

Transfer the paste to a large mixing bowl and pour in the olive oil in a thin stream, stirring, until just mixed.

Chapter 6

Make Mine Hot

From eggs and fried chicken to ramen and a Bloody Mary, there's a recipe with hot sauce for everyone.

Scrambled Eggs with Hot Sauce

You could just shake some hot sauce over fried eggs, but try this recipe for a real treat.

    2 large eggs
    1 tablespoon light cream
    1 teaspoon sriracha sauce, or to taste
    Salt and ground black pepper, to taste
    2 tablespoons butter

Beat the eggs in a bowl with all the ingredients, except the butter.

Melt the butter in a nonstick saucepan over medium-low heat, tilting the pan to coat the bottom. Pour the egg mixture into the pan and cook, stirring occasionally, for 3 to 5 minutes, or until the eggs are set to your preference.

Mexican Ranch-Style Eggs

An easy breakfast to whip up that makes the classic Valentina red hot sauce the hero. If you can't find this brand, use Cholula.

2 small flour tortillas
2 tablespoons vegetable oil
1 firm medium tomato, sliced
3 tablespoons red Valentina sauce
Pinch of dried oregano
Pat of butter

2 eggs
½ avocado, pitted and diced
Monterey Jack cheese, shredded
Fresh cilantro, chopped

Dry-fry the tortillas in a skillet; keep warm. Heat the oil in a saucepan and fry the tomato slices for a minute on each side. Add the hot sauce and oregano. Stir for a minute; set aside. Melt the butter in a skillet over medium-low heat and fry the eggs.

Place an egg on each tortilla; top with the tomatoes, avocado, cheese, and cilantro.

George Jessel's Pick-Me-Up

This Bloody Mary recipe appeared in Charlie Connelly's *The World Famous Cotton Club: 1939 Book of Mixed Drinks,* perhaps evidence of Jessel's claim to have invented the cocktail.

2 fl ounces (60 ml) vodka
6 fl ounces (180 ml) tomato juice
2 dashes Tabasco sauce
Juice of ½ lemon

Shake the ingredients together with ice, then pour into a tall glass.

Bloody Mary Day

Today, you can use a Bloody Mary mix first produced by the McIlhenny Company in 1976 to make the cocktail, which you can enjoy on Bloody Mary Day, which is (unofficially) on January 1. You might need one after taking your New Year's dip if you're a member of the Polar Bear Club.

Virgin Mary

You can add additional ingredients, such as horseradish, wasabi, ground ginger, paprika, garlic powder, or nutmeg—or experiment and make your own concoction!

3 fl ounces (90 ml) good-quality tomato juice
1 tablespoon lemon juice
1 dash Worcestershire sauce
1 teaspoon celery salt
2 dashes Tabasco sauce
1 stalk celery, to garnish

Fill a tall glass with ice cubes, then pour in the tomato juice and lemon juice. Mix well. Add the remaining ingredients, garnishing with the celery stalk.

Perhaps the least healthy choice, but sometimes unavoidable—at times, just a little of last night's poison does the trick.

Gwyneth Paltrow, actress,
on her hangover cure—a Bloody Mary

Rihanna's Mac and Cheese

The Barbadian singer-songwriter has spread her wings beyond the music scene and into the world of recipes. Her recipe for mac and cheese has some unusual ingredients. It's not the sautéed vegetables added to cooked macaroni that have her fans excited, but the cheese sauce with a twist—as well as mustard and ketchup, it includes a Jamaican Scotch bonnet hot sauce.

Spice Up Your Mac and Cheese

The next time you make your favorite macaroni and cheese, add a dash or two of Tabasco sauce—just like the TV chef Julia Child. For a milder taste, add the hot sauce along with the cheese in the cooking method. Taste and add more if it's not spicy enough.

Buffalo Sauce

Use this sauce for dipping or as a base for other recipes.

¼ cup (60 ml) Frank's RedHot sauce
4 tablespoons (60 g) butter
1½ teaspoons distilled white vinegar
⅛ teaspoon cayenne pepper
Pinch of garlic powder
¼ teaspoon Worcestershire sauce
Salt, to taste

Add the hot sauce with the butter, vinegar, cayenne pepper, garlic powder, Worcestershire sauce, and salt to a saucepan over low heat, and simmer, stirring occasionally, until the butter is melted.

Buffalo Chicken Wings

These favorites wouldn't be the same without a healthy dose of spicy sauce.

    Vegetable oil, for deep-frying
    16 chicken wings
    Buffalo Sauce (see recipe opposite)

In a deep fryer or pot, heat the oil to 375°F (190°C) and fry the wings, in batches, for about 15 minutes, until golden and crispy. Drain well.

Toss the wings in the sauce and bake in a preheated oven, at 300°F (150°C/Gas Mark 2) for 5 minutes.

Buffalo Cauliflower

A vegan substitute for chicken wings.

Cooking oil spray
½ cup (60 g) flour
½ cup (125 ml) water
2 teaspoons garlic powder
1 teaspoon paprika
1 head cauliflower, cut into florets
Buffalo Sauce (see page 174)
Salt and ground black pepper, to taste

Preheat the oven to 450°F (230°C/Gas Mark 8). Spray cooking oil on a baking sheet and line with parchment paper.

In a bowl, whisk the flour, water, garlic powder, paprika, salt, and black pepper to a smooth batter. Add the cauliflower and toss to coat.

Bake for 20 to 25 minutes, turning over halfway through. Brush with the Buffalo Sauce. Bake for another 15 minutes.

Increase the Heat

When using a Louisiana-style sauce, you add tanginess as well as heat when you use more. If you only want a hotter result, then simply add ½ teaspoon or more of cayenne powder, depending on the recipe. It's best to add a minimum amount at first and taste, before adding more. This is true for any sauce—always use the least amount, taste, then add more, if necessary.

Spice Up Your Condiments

Hot sauce can be added to a number of condiments to add a punch of heat. Add your favorite hot sauce to:

Hollandaise sauce

Tartar sauce

Vinaigrette salad dressing

Ketchup and mayo, for a thousand island-style dressing

Mayonnaise, to create a spicy dip

Melted butter, to drizzle over popcorn

Chutney, for a sweet and spicy hit

Mustard, for a spicy hot dog

Simple syrup, to toss with a fruit salad

66

First you bring the sugar, then you bring the hot sauce.

99

Kevin Ollie, basketball coach and player

Louisiana-style Margarita Cocktail

Nothing goes better with tequila and lime than a hit of chili.

- 1 lime wedge
- 1 teaspoon sugar
- 2 tablespoons (30 ml) tequila
- 2 tablespoons (30 ml) triple sec
- 2 tablespoons (30 ml) lime juice
- 1 dash Louisiana-style hot sauce

Rub a lime wedge around the rim of a margarita glass. Place the sugar in a saucer and dip the rim of the glass.

Fill a cocktail shaker halfway with cracked ice, then add the tequila, triple sec, lime juice, any remaining sugar, and hot sauce. Shake well and strain into the glass.

Ramen Stir-Fry

The perfect way to complement a healthy noodle supper—
feel free to add vegetables like bok choi, mushrooms, and
seaweed, or protein such as tofu, chicken, or shrimp.

    2 tablespoons sesame oil
    2 scallions, sliced, white and green parts separated
    2 cloves garlic, minced
    1 teaspoon minced garlic
    3 cups cooked ramen noodles
    2 tablespoons soy sauce
    1 tablespoon rice vinegar
    1 tablespoon sriracha

Heat the oil in a large saucepan over medium heat. Add the white
parts of the scallions and sauté for 2 minutes, until soft. Add the garlic
and sauté for 1 minute.

Add the noodles and toss to mix, then add the remaining ingredients,
toss together, and cook for about 2 minutes to heat through.

Cajun Seasoning

A typical cajun blend of salt, paprika, onion powder, garlic powder, and white pepper can be spiced up with the addition of crushed dried chilies. Use it as a dry rub for meat, add it to gumbo or jambalaya, or put it in the coating for your fried chicken or fish.

Spicy Glazed Chicken

For best results, marinate the chicken overnight so the flavors can develop.

- ⅓ cup (75 ml) Louisiana-style hot sauce
- ¼ cup (60 ml) honey
- 1 tablespoon lime juice
- 1 tablespoon soy sauce
- 4 boneless, skinless chicken breasts or thighs, halved lengthwise

In a large bowl, mix the hot sauce with the honey, lime juice, and soy sauce. Add the chicken and coat with the marinade. Cover with plastic wrap and marinate in the refrigerator for at least 30 minutes, but preferably overnight.

Grill the chicken in a skillet over medium heat for 15 minutes, turning and basting halfway through, until the meat is cooked through and the juices run clear.

Sambal Chicken Skewers

An Asian sticky chicken dish that can also be cooked on an outdoor grill.

½ cup (100 g) packed light brown sugar
½ cup (125 ml) rice vinegar
5 tablespoons sambal oelek or other hot chili paste
¼ cup (60 ml) Thai fish sauce
¼ cup (60 ml) sriracha
2 teaspoons grated fresh ginger
4 skinless, boneless chicken thighs, cut into 2-inch (5-cm) pieces

Whisk all the ingredients, except the chicken, in a bowl. Add the chicken and toss to coat.

Thread the chicken onto wooden skewers soaked in water for 30 minutes. Bring the remaining marinade to a boil in a saucepan, then simmer for about 10 minutes, until reduced by half.

Grill the chicken, turning and basting with the marinade, for 8 to 10 minutes, until cooked through.

Spicy Pork Tenderloin

Sambal oelek is thicker and less processed than sriracha and doesn't contain sugar, so the chili flavors are more enhanced.

    2 tablespoons sambal oelek or sriracha
    2 tablespoons soy sauce
    2 tablespoons brown sugar
    10-inch (25-cm) piece fresh ginger, finely grated
    1 clove garlic, minced
    1½ pounds (675 g) pork tenderloin, thinly sliced
    Vegetable oil

Add all the ingredients, except the pork and oil, to a jar, seal with the lid, and shake. Pour the sauce over the pork and marinate in the fridge for 30 minutes to 1 hour.

Heat the oil in a skillet over high heat. When hot, add the pork, in batches, in a single layer. Sear for 1 to 2 minutes on each side, until golden brown.

Spicy Grilled Cheese Sandwich

1 tablespoon butter
2 slices white bread
2 slices Gouda cheese
1 slice tomato
Cholula hot sauce, to taste

Butter one side of each slice of bread. Place a cheese slice on top of the unbuttered side of one bread slice, add the tomato and a dash or so of hot sauce, then the second cheese slice and remaining bread slice, butter side up.

Cook the sandwich in a skillet over medium heat for about 5 minutes, until the cheese melts and the bread is golden brown, then flip with a spatula and cook the second side for a few minutes.

Spicy Grilled Cheese Variations

- Use a different type of cheese, such as Cheddar or Monterey Jack.
- Use another type of bread, such as whole-wheat or sourdough.
- Replace the tomato with caramelized sliced onion, bacon, spinach, or mashed avocado.
- Try a different hot sauce, such as a homemade Buffalo Sauce (see page 174).

Sriracha Grilled Tofu

A fiery, flavorful vegan choice as a main or side dish.

   1 cup (250 ml) sriracha sauce
   1 tablespoon soy sauce
   1 tablespoon rice wine vinegar
   2 teaspoons garlic powder
   1 teaspoon ground black pepper
   1 teaspoon ground ginger
   12-ounce (350-g) package extra-firm tofu, cut into cubes

Combine all the ingredients, except the tofu in a medium bowl, then add the tofu and toss to coat. Cover and marinate for 1 hour or overnight in the refrigerator.

Grill for 2 to 3 minutes on each side, brushing with extra sauce.

Easy Mexican Shrimp Cocktail

To vary this dish, add diced cucumber or chopped celery, or omit the tomato sauce and ketchup.

    1 pound (450 g) peeled, cooked shrimp
    ½ red onion, minced
    1 cup (160 g) diced tomatoes
    1 cup (250 g) tomato sauce
    ¼ cup (70 g) ketchup
    1 avocado, pitted and diced
    ¼ cup (10 g) chopped fresh cilantro
    2 tablespoons lime juice
    2 teaspoons Tapatío or Cholula hot sauce
    1 tablespoon olive oil
    Salt and pepper, to taste

Put all the ingredients into a bowl and mix gently. Spoon into glasses and serve immediately, or refrigerate, covered, for up to 2 hours.

Easy Chili Con Carne

Using Frank's RedHot sauce makes a spicier version of this quick family meal.

2 pounds (900 g) ground beef
1 onion, chopped
3 cups (750 g) crushed tomatoes
2½ cups (425 g) red kidney beans
¼ cup (60 ml) Frank's RedHot sauce
2 tablespoons chili powder
2 teaspoons cumin
½ teaspoon cayenne pepper
½ teaspoon garlic powder
Salt and pepper, to taste

Cook the beef in a large saucepan over medium heat for about 5 minutes, until browned. Add the onion and cook for 3 minutes. Drain.

Add the remaining ingredients, increase the heat, and bring to a boil. Reduce the heat to medium and simmer, stirring occasionally, for about 15 minutes.

White Fish with Zhug

The green zhug it is a popular condiment for falafel and shawarma, and traditionally served with hummus in the Middle East.

    2 fillets halibut, red snapper, or other white fish
    1 tablespoon olive oil
    1 tablespoon lemon juice
    2 tablespoons zhug (see page 163)
    Salt and ground black pepper, to taste

Preheat the oven to 400°F (200°C/Gas Mark 6) .

Put the fish fillets into a lined baking pan, skin side up, and drizzle with the olive oil and lemon juice. Season, then bake for 10 to 12 minutes, until the fish easily flakes apart. Serve hot, accompanied by the zhug.

> ❝
>
> *Hot sauce must be hot. If you don't like it hot, use less.*
>
> ❞

David Tran, creator of Huy Fong sriracha